Heavenly Fire

The life and ministry of
William Grimshaw of Haworth (1708–1763)

by Esther Bennett

W: Grimshaw—

Introduction

To judge by the shock-wave, which could still be felt, I think, well into this century, [William Grimshaw] struck the whole region 'like a planet'," writes the twentieth-century poet, Ted Hughes, in notes to his poetry collection, *Remains of Elmet*.[1] The colossal impact of the eighteenth-century curate of Haworth on the surrounding area of West Yorkshire is now largely forgotten. Most visitors to Haworth today are following in the footsteps of the Brontë sisters, and will know of William Grimshaw only from Elizabeth Gaskell's whimsical description in her famous life of Charlotte Brontë (1816–1855).[2] Yet the nineteenth-century Haworth in which the Brontës lived and wrote was essentially the product of the ministry of Grimshaw. One of his earliest biographers writes of a visit to Haworth in 1826, "Everything bears the imprint of his name, bears the stamp of his character, zeal and labours."[3]

Born in Lancashire in 1708, William Grimshaw was educated at Christ's College, Cambridge, from 1726 to 1731, and returned north to take up holy orders in Yorkshire, first briefly at Littleborough, then at Todmorden, and then for over twenty years in Haworth. Although he was initially influenced by Deism,[4] and was characterized by a dissipated lifestyle, Grimshaw's religious conversion in 1741 had a revolutionary effect on his own life and ministry and on the lives of his parishioners. He became closely identified with John Wesley (1703–1791) and other leaders of the Evangelical Revival. This grass-roots religious awakening within the Church of England eventually led to the founding of the Methodist church in England and the Calvinistic Methodist denomination in Wales. Although rated by the nineteenth-century writer and Anglican cleric, J.C. Ryle, as one of the three greatest churchmen of the eighteenth century—alongside John Wesley and George Whitefield (1714–1770)—Grimshaw has remained less well known because of a lack of early biographical material and because his work was largely confined to the north of England.[5]

William Grimshaw was appointed curate of St. Michael and All Angels in 1742, the same post Patrick Brontë was to hold years later. Pictured is the Haworth church as it stands today.

chapter 1

A worldly cleric

Born at Brindle in Lancashire in 1708 into a humble family, William Grimshaw showed early intellectual promise, and entered Christ's College, Cambridge, in 1726 at the age of seventeen. Christ's College, which could boast the seventeenth-century poet and pamphleteer John Milton (1608–1674) among its former students, took in only nine other freshmen with Grimshaw. Despite its reputation, academic standards at Cambridge at this time were at a low ebb. The majority of the fellows preferred to leave the lecturing to the tutors and academic requirements for completing a degree course were minimal. As John Wesley acerbically remarked, "the moment a young man sets foot in either Oxford or Cambridge he is surrounded by company of all kinds...with loungers and triflers of every sort; with men who no more concern themselves with learning than religion."[6]

After a year or two of self-

John Newton

John Newton, Anglican minister and celebrated hymn-writer, was dramatically converted from a dissolute life in 1747. During his stay in Liverpool from 1755 onwards, he made the aquaintance of William Grimshaw. In later years he exercised a notable ministry that made him a key figure in Evangelical circles in the last quarter of the eighteenth century. When visiting Haworth in 1758, Newton records in his diary: "Had it been the will of God, methought I could have rencounced the world to have lived in these mountains with such a minister, and such a people...." Newton was the first important biographer of Grimshaw.

Your sincere friend & servant John Newton

discipline during which Grimshaw described himself as "sober and diligent," he succumbed to the prevailing customs and, on his own admission, learned to drink and swear and became as vile as the worst of his fellow students.[7]

Here, too, in this centre of ideas, Grimshaw encountered, possibly for the first time, the great Enlightenment thinkers. The prominence which they gave to logic or reason, with or (increasingly) without God as the supreme being, was affecting religious thought throughout the upper and middle classes. Particularly influential was *The Reasonableness of Christianity* (1685), a book by John Locke (1632–1704) which attempted, with reason as the touchstone, to defend a simple "biblical" religion without resort to creed or tradition. The philosophical movement known as Deism went further by discounting revelation itself. Christianity was presented as a religion in which God as the creator or First Cause had set the world in motion and then left it to its own devices.

At the end of his time at Cambridge Grimshaw sought ordination in the Church of England. The usual motive, he acknowledged, was of "getting a good living, a curacy or bread. I confess it was mine."[8] His deistic views and dissolute lifestyle, far from disqualifying him, reflected that of many of the Anglican clergy of the day. Yet returning north to a curacy, first in Littleborough for a few months, and then in nearby Todmorden, he took pains to conceal his worldly lifestyle, "rightly judging," as he later relates, "that his friends would think their money ill-bestowed, if they saw him an accomplished rake."[9] With God's revelation denied, God's authority over moral behaviour could be safely ignored.

For three years, Grimshaw spent his days hunting and fishing, and his evenings socialising with the influential members of society, gambling, drinking and swearing. John Newton (1725–1807), his friend of later years recounts, "He did his duty, as the phrase is, in the church, once on the Lord's day. With this his conscience was satisfied. Whether his flock was satisfied, he neither knew nor cared."[10]

chapter 2

A transformed man: Grimshaw's religious conversion

William Grimshaw's awareness of the sin in his life came in 1734, and it was sudden and outwardly inexplicable. Perhaps the bereavement suffered by two of his parishioners at the death of their baby daughter combined with his own inability to comfort the distraught mother, who continued to dress and tend her dead child, shook his complacency. "Put away all gloomy thoughts, and go into merry company and divert yourselves and all will soon be right" was his advice.[11] When they returned, unhelped, seeking further counsel, Grimshaw acknowledged his own spiritual bankruptcy. "To despair of the mercy of God would be the worst thing of all" was the only comment he could make.[12]

From this point on, Grimshaw sought to reform his own lifestyle. Instead of the pleasant daily recreation and the nightly carousing, he kept a strict record of all his sins, balancing them against his good deeds. He dutifully visited all his parishioners, catechised the children, and urged reformation of life on them as well as himself. Yet satisfying the rigours of God's standards seemed impossible. Such was his depression of spirits that on one Sunday he felt hardly able to mount the steps of the pulpit. In despair, he would preach to his congregation: "My friends, we are in a damnable state, and I scarcely know how we are to get out of it."[13]

Now the deistic notions that he had imbibed during Cambridge days presented fresh problems to his faith. He was "tempted often to blaspheme…to believe that Christ was a mere man; [and] to undervalue and despise the work of creation as being no more than for a man to make a top or any little machine."[14] About this time, two of his parishioners attempted to commit suicide, one by hanging and the other by cutting his throat. Grimshaw was called to visit the latter. His first reflection, he recalls, was "Hah! I don't know how soon I may do this too."[15]

This spiritual struggle continued for some years. Early in 1741 an incident occurred that finally brought relief from his mental and spiritual anguish. This was the discovery of a book, lying on a table at a friend's house, by the seventeenth-century Puritan divine, John Owen (1616–1683), called *The Doctrine of Justification by Faith* (1677). In it, Owen expounded the biblical teaching of the imputed righteousness of Christ. Owen demonstrated from the New Testament that the person who had received Christ's righteousness by believing in his death for sinners no longer needed to strive to make himself acceptable to God. Instead he was counted by God as possessing the obedience and righteousness of Christ without needing any contribution of his own.

Already convinced of his own shortcomings, this was sweet music to Grimshaw's ears: "I was now willing to renounce myself, every degree of fancied merit and ability, and to embrace Christ

Nestled in the rugged hills of West Yorkshire, Haworth today is mostly remembered as the home and haunts of the literary Brontë sisters. Unknown to many, it was also the location of a great spiritual awakening in the North of England in the eighteenth century.

only for my all in all. O what light and comfort did I now enjoy in my own soul, and what a taste of the pardoning love of God!"[16] "Heaven in the soul," was how he later described those days. "His Bible became a new book to him," one contemporary records. "Yea, he told me, that if God had drawn up his Bible to heaven, and sent him down another, it could not have been newer to him."[17]

Unknown to William Grimshaw, similar conversion experiences were happening in the lives of others who were to play a major role in the Evangelical Revival. A plaque still marks the spot in Aldersgate Street near the Barbican Centre in London where on May 24, 1738, John Wesley had his "heart strangely warmed" and he "did trust in Christ, Christ alone for salvation."[18] Others recorded similar life-changing experiences.

Aspects of Grimshaw's ministry now began to change. Extempore prayers were now mixed with the liturgy. The sermons, previously dominated by themes of sin and judgement, now contained offers of forgiveness and peace.

PHOTO BY PENNY DICKSON

chapter 3

Early ministry in Haworth 1742–1745

In May 1742, William Grimshaw was appointed curate of St. Michael and All Angels in Haworth. Having now been brought into an understanding of justification by faith, Grimshaw's ambition was no longer to fulfil the minimal requirements of his clerical office, but to bring a transforming message to other eternal souls who were lost, as his own soul had been.

Character of Haworth

Journeying through the West Riding in 1726, the novelist and journalist Daniel Defoe (1660–1731) observed the thriving textile industry that provided occupation for the entire family in almost every house he passed. A century later, the public health inspector, William Herschell Babbage, pointed out "the close and unhealthy conditions" that this occasioned in the home. Babbage's report also exposed the low standards of hygiene. In Haworth, like most other towns in this area, refuse from shops and houses ran down the centre of the street. Mortality rates in Haworth were as high as in Whitechapel and the most unhealthy districts of London.[19]

Drinking, gambling and violence appear to have been the principal diversions, palliatives from overwork and the ever-present threat of disease. The historian, J.H. Plumb, comments that "in every class [there was] the same taut neurotic quality—the fantastic gambling and drinking, the riots, brutality and violence, and everywhere and always a constant sense of death."[20] The Established Church, having rationalized away sin and guilt and supernatural intervention under the impact of Deism, now appeared irrelevant to the average working man. "It was not a religion which had much appeal to the men and women living brutal, squalid lives. …They needed revelation and salvation."[21]

Recalling his early days in the parish, William Grimshaw commented: "When I first came into this country, if I had gone half a day's journey on horseback towards the east, west, north or south, I could not meet or hear of one truly serious person."[22] The inhabitants "had little more sense of religion than their cattle," affirms Grimshaw's biographer, John Newton, "and were wild and uneducated like the mountains and rocks which surrounded them."[23]

Early labours in the parish

Now having a positive message to deliver, Grimshaw's first task was to install a new pulpit in the church. Two verses of Scripture he had engraved on the sounding board above the three-tiered pulpit can still be read: "I am determined to know nothing among you, save Jesus Christ and him crucified" (1 Corinthians 2:2) and "For to me, to live is Christ, and to die is gain" (Philippians 1:21), a verse which was to be the touchstone of his subsequent ministry in Haworth.

The preaching that Grimshaw's

parishioners heard echoed these sentiments. Appealing to his hearers' consciences, he denounced their sin, warned of the dire consequences of continuing in it, and urged them to accept Christ as their only hope of salvation. None of Grimshaw's sermons survive, but his unpublished treatise "The Admonition of a Sinner" gives a flavour of his sermonic style:

> My neighbour, my friend, my heart longs over you. Your manner of life is actually, openly and evidently such that if not seasonably prevented, it will shortly and certainly terminate in your inevitable, intolerable, eternal ruin and destruction. …Don't be angry with me, please don't. It's because I love you that I thus address you. …I want you without delay to repent of your sins, "to seek the Lord while he may be found, to call upon him while he is near"(Isaiah 55:6). Acquaint yourself with him, be at peace with him, through his blood, that thereby good may come to you: pardon, peace, grace, heaven, glory, glory for evermore.[24]

The empty pews began to fill as people, not just from Haworth but from the surrounding area, were touched by this passionate message that brought hope of personal salvation. Despite his own academic background, Grimshaw spoke in what he termed "market language."[25] Familiar stories of the Bible were conveyed to his listeners using graphic, every-day imagery. Speaking of the Prodigal Son, one of his hearers recalls him suddenly pointing and calling out: "Yonder he comes! Yonder he comes, all in rags. Yonder he comes, rag, tag, and bobtail."[26] On another occasion, in despair at the unresponsiveness of his congregation, he exclaimed: "I may talk to you till my tongue is as small as a sparble [a small nail used by cobblers] but you will go to hell after all!"[27] The older people he would affectionately refer to as "old moss-crops."[28]

The relevance of the message was becoming apparent to the listeners. "A few souls were affected under the word, brought to see their lost estate by nature, and to experience peace through the blood of Jesus," reported Grimshaw of these first months in Haworth.[29]

When the Archbishop of York, Thomas Herring (1693–1757), visited the parish in June 1743, Grimshaw reported that the number of communicants had risen from an average of twelve to between fifty and sixty. The actual congregation far outnumbered this. By the end of 1742 it had become obvious that the church would need to be enlarged. An application for permission to enlarge the building was granted the following year, although because the money for the project had to be raised by Haworth parish itself, it was a further ten years before the enlargement was completed.

Grimshaw did not limit his duties to the church services. For the very poor, who cited their "vile cloaths" as an excuse for not attending the church, Grimshaw arranged a weekly service in his parsonage, "Sowdens," on Sunday evenings. If others of his parishioners were disinclined to attend, it was not uncommon for them to discover that Grimshaw had arranged a service in their own home for the following week. "I know I am not welcome," he would bluntly admit, "but I will speak to every one under my care concerning his soul. If you will not come and hear, you shall hear me at home: and if you perish, you will perish wi' t' sound o' t' gospel i' yer lugs!"[30]

In the summer of 1743 he divided the three hundred families in the parish into twelve societies. He visited three families in each society each month, thus beginning what he called "my monthly visitations."

Assurance of salvation, September 1744

Grimshaw himself had a further notable experience in the autumn of 1744 that gave fresh momentum and confidence to his ministry. Writing autobiographically, he recorded that we may shortly after conversion "think that we are not God's child, that we are not justified nor pardoned, that we are mistaken with ourselves."[31]

This period of self-doubting came suddenly to an end. During a Sunday morning service in September 1744, Grimshaw was overcome by physical weakness and had to be taken to the nearby Black Bull Inn, whose proprietor, Jonathan Whitehead, was the parish clerk. While the servants were trying to revive him, he later described to a friend how he fell into a strange trance-like state, in which he believed himself to be in "a dark foul passage," and to be overhearing God the Father conferring with God the Son about the eternal destiny of Grimshaw's soul. Seized with acute anxiety, he feared the prospect looked bleak until he saw the Lord Jesus showing his wounded hands and feet, and he was joyfully reassured of his personal acceptance before God. "I have had a glorious vision from the third heaven" was Grimshaw's only comment at the time, but from that point on he was free from debilitating spiritual doubt.[32]

Within the eighteen months that followed he records "six score souls believing in Christ." The church was crowded to capacity, and he sometimes had to resort to addressing the overflowing congregations from the graveyard.

The Black Bull Inn where Grimshaw was taken to be revived after being overcome in the pulpit in 1744.

PHOTO BY PENNY DICKSON

An experience of Grimshaw

The best account I have met with of the incident to which Mr. Grimshaw refers on Sept. 2, 1744, and which I think may be credited, was given by a person who then lived with him as a servant, to the following purport: "That she was called up that morning at five o'clock, but found her master was risen before her, and was retired into a private room for prayer. After remaining there some time, he went to a house in Haworth, where he was engaged a while in religious exercises with some of his people, he then returned home and retired for prayer again and from thence to church. She believes he had not eaten any thing that morning. While reading the second lesson he fell down; he was soon helped up and led out of the church. He continued to talk to the people as he went, and desired them not to disperse, for he hoped he should return to them soon, and he had something extraordinary to say to them. They led him to the clerk's house where he lay seemingly insensible. She, with others, were employed in rubbing his limbs (which were exceedingly cold) with warm cloths. After some time he came to himself, and seemed to be in great rapture. The first words he spoke were: "I have had a glorious vision from the third heaven." But she does not remember that he made any mention of what he had seen. In the afternoon he performed service in the church which began at two o'clock, and preached and spoke so long to the people, that it was seven in the evening before he returned home." So far the testimony of his servant.

Newton, *Memoirs*, 30–32.

chapter 4

Years of expansion 1746–1754

By the time Joseph Williams (1692–1755), a merchant from Kidderminster with a keen interest in spiritual renewal, visited Haworth in the spring of 1746, Grimshaw was preaching to congregations of between a thousand and twelve hundred people. Barely three years later George Whitefield, one of the best known itinerant preachers of the Evangelical Revival, preached for Grimshaw at Haworth. "At Mr. Grimshaw's," he records in a letter, "I believe there were about six thousand hearers. The sacramental occasion was most awful [awesome]."[33] "What a sacrament at Haworth!" he writes of a later visit. "We used thirty-five bottles of wine."[34]

Joseph Williams noted the transformation that occurred in the lives of many of Grimshaw's parishioners from this time. "Families in which sin had made the most miserable havoc, and in which all the comforts of life were destroyed, now were made happy in the fear of God."[35] People worked harder, and maintained their families better. Grimshaw developed a close knowledge of his parishioners by regularly visiting the "societies." He continually asked them to attend the preaching, and if such exhortations failed, he resorted to more unconventional means to ensure their attendance. On one such occasion, in disguise, he joined a group of wayward young people out on the moors on a Sunday night. With hands joined in a circle, one young man recognized with dismay the familiar legs of the curate, and raising his eyes found his fears confirmed! The majority of the group were found in church the following Sunday!

"Beyond bounds"

Success brought tensions. As a committed minister of the Church of England, Grimshaw felt bound to operate within the protocol of that body. This included, among other things, ministering within parish boundaries. The worldly apathy, however, of neighbouring clergymen left their parishioners to continue hell-bound, in Grimshaw's view, without any message of salvation. People already flocked to Haworth from up to twenty miles away to hear him preaching. Against his own better judgement, the urgent requests of individuals frequently induced him to break the regulations and venture beyond the bounds of his own parish. Eventually, in 1747, "affected," in his own words, "with strong impressions to preach the gospel abroad" he abandoned these scruples.[36] He now embarked on an itinerant ministry, a prototype of what eventually became known as the "Great Haworth Round."

The exhausting spiritual demands of the Haworth revival led him to make another innovation against his principles as a good churchman—from 1745 he began to use lay preachers. He soon had a small band of assistants, familiarly known as 'Mr.

PHOTO (OPPOSITE PAGE) BY JANICE VAN ECK

Grimshaw's men" and who were fired with the same fervour. "I hope your love abides in full strength," he wrote to one of his young helpers, Thomas Lee (1727–1786), "and that you preach twenty times a week. ...Preaching is health, food and physic to me and why not to thee, my brother?"[37]

Disorder and unrest stirred up by resentful local clergymen, frequently accompanied Grimshaw and his men. In May 1748, Grimshaw was called to account for his activities to the newly appointed Archbishop of York, Matthew Hutton (1693–1758). On hearing of the large numbers that attended the quarterly sacraments, Hutton phlegmatically concluded: "We cannot find fault with Mr. Grimshaw, as he is instrumental in bringing such numbers to the Lord's Table."[38]

At the parsonage, "Sowdens"—now a working farm—a plaque records the visits of "John and Charles Wesley, George Whitefield, John Newton, Henry Venn."

The experience of Thomas Lee

In the year 1752, and during the winter following, the work of God prospered exceedingly; but persecution raged on every side.…One day, as I was going through Pateley [Bridge], the captain of the mob [there], who was kept in constant pay, pursued me, and pulled me off my horse. The mob then soon collected about me; and…dragged me into a house by the hair of the head; then pushed me back, with one or two upon me, and threw me with the small of my back upon the edge of the stone stairs. This nearly broke my back; and it was not well for many years after. Thence they dragged me to the common sewer, which carries the dirt of the town to the river. They rolled me in it for some time; then dragged me to the bridge and threw me into the water. They had me mostly on the ground, my strength being quite spent.

My wife, with some friends, now came up. Seeing her busy about me, some asked: "What, are you a Methodist?"—gave her several blows which made her bleed at the mouth, and swore they would put her into the river. All this time I lay upon the ground, the mob being undetermined what to do. Some cried out: "Make an end of him"—others were for sparing my life; but the dispute was cut short by their agreeing to put some others into the water. So they took them away, leaving me and my wife together. She endeavoured to raise me up; but, having no strength, I dropped to the ground again, and [she] supported me about a hundred yards; then I was set on horseback, and made a shift to ride softly as far as Michael Granger's house. Here I was stripped from head to foot, and was washed. I left my wet clothes here, and rode to Greenhow Hill, where many were waiting for me; and though much bruised and very weak, preached a short sermon from Psalm xxxiv.19: "Many are the troubles of the righteous; but the Lord delivereth him out of them all."

Cragg, *Grimshaw of Haworth*, 78-79

(clockwise from top left) George Whitefield, Charles Wesley, John Wesley and Selina Hastings, the Countess of Huntingdon

These four central figures in the grass-roots revival of the eighteenth century were, like Grimshaw, gripped by a passion to spread real Christianity throughout the length and breadth of the British Isles and into the New World. Both Whitefield and the Wesley brothers preached at the Haworth church during Grimshaw's day and saw great numbers come to salvation in Christ. Lady Huntingdon was a friend of Grimshaw's and an encouraging and generous supporter of the work of these evangelists in bringing the Gospel to needy men and women.

Connection with the Evangelical Revival

Grimshaw's early ministry in Haworth was at first isolated from the spiritual awakening that was occurring in other parts of the country under the leadership of the Wesley brothers and George Whitefield. Indeed in one of Grimshaw's early meetings with Charles Wesley in 1747, he cautiously arranged for Wesley to preach not in his own church, but in a local hall. Before long, however, it became evident that their message was the same and Haworth became a northern preaching centre for all the main revival leaders. For one of Whitefield's visits new pewter communion flagons were made to hold the extra communion wine that would be needed.[39] From 1747 John Wesley put Grimshaw in charge of his "northern round" of societies and in 1749 he nominated Grimshaw as his successor in the leadership of Methodism (still a movement within the Church of England) in the event of his death and that of his brother, Charles.

chapter 5

Years of consolation 1755–1763

The Great Haworth Round

Over the years, the vast and unwieldy "northern" circuit for which Grimshaw assumed responsibility in 1747 was broken down into more manageable areas. Grimshaw divided the "Haworth round," which extended from Cockermouth in the north to Birstall in the south, into two circuits that he visited on alternate weeks. These he playfully termed "my idle week" and "my busy week" as he might preach an average of fifteen times in the former compared with nearly double that in the "busy week." "What has God wrought in the midst of those rough mountains!" John Wesley exclaimed after spending a day or two on the Haworth Round in 1761.[40]

The procedure Grimshaw normally followed on his pastoral visits is best described in the words of one of his hearers. "His usual manner was, upon entering the house, after having with uplifted hands pronounced a blessing upon the people assembled, to fall down upon his knees and pray with great fervency, and then preach with a plainness and pungency peculiarly adapted to his hearers, for a convenient space of time."[41]

Indefatigable labours

"I live at Haworth when I am at home, and when I am abroad, I am abroad; but at home or abroad my work is the same; 'Tis to preach Jesus and him crucified; and to help, thro' him, poor sinners to God, grace and glory." Thus simply Grimshaw assessed his life's work in a letter to his friend and fellow minister, William Romaine (1714–1795), in 1761.[42] He employed his singular physical strength and stamina to their limits to achieve his goal. "He used his body with less compassion than a merciful man would use his beast," Henry Venn (1724–1797) observed at his funeral service in 1763.[43] "Lord, grant that I may not faint,"

Henry Venn (above) and William Romaine (below)

Though not as well known as Whitefield and Wesley, Henry Venn and William Romaine were important Evangelical preachers in their day and personal friends of Grimshaw. Venn preached Grimshaw's funeral sermon.

Grimshaw prayed, "till weakness, old age or death invalidate me. By the grace of God, I'm resolved never to flag while I can ride, walk, creep or crawl!"[44]

Consolidation in Haworth

The extension of the church for which Grimshaw had obtained permission in 1743 was finally completed in 1755. Even this was not adequate to hold the crowds that flocked to hear George Whitefield later that year. The following year, as a necessary expedient, Grimshaw rigged up a scaffolding pulpit familiarly known at "Mr Whitefield's pulpit," enabling the preacher to emerge from the church through a window and preach from the vantage point of this raised platform to the crowds thronging the graveyard below.

Church or Dissent

As time went on, it became increasingly difficult to contain the vibrant spiritual life of Methodism within the Established Church. More staunch a churchman than many of the revival leaders, Grimshaw himself had breached a number of the church's regulations. Yet he remained convinced that the doctrines of Methodism were consistent with the Church of England, and he abhorred all unnecessary erosion of the church's authority, such as the suggestion that unordained men should dispense the Lord's Supper. "I am determined to live and die in close communion a member and minister of the Church of England," he avowed.[45]

This did not, however, prevent Grimshaw from building a small preaching house in Haworth in 1758 to provide an alternative base for his congregation if the next incumbent after his death

The testimony of William Crabtree

When I was about seventeen years of age [in 1737], I became my own master. I was boarded in a wicked village, next door to hell itself.... I was linked in company with five or six young men who did all in their power to teach me all manner of wickedness: to do which, I thought was very manly. I thought I was too young to learn, but through custom it became habitual.... About that time [the 1740s] Mr. Grimshaw, of Haworth, came into the neighbourhood to preach. I was requested to go and hear him. I thought I would not, but this thought passed my mind:—"Go, it can do thee no harm." So I went to hear him. He was preaching about "the Prodigal Son." He made this observation, "that one sin would damn a soul as well as a thousand." It struck me to the heart. I thought my case deplorable: I went after that to Haworth constantly to hear him.

Isaac Mann, *Memoirs of the Rev. Wm. Crabtree, First Pastor of the Baptist Church at Bradford, Yorkshire* (London: Button and Son, 1815), 12–14.

should fail to meet the spiritual needs of the people. Carved in a tablet on the wall were the words of his life-long motto: "For us to live is Christ, to die is gain, AD 1758." The meeting-house was seldom used, however, during Grimshaw's lifetime.

In contrast to many of his time, Grimshaw displayed an eclectic sympathy for all who preached the Biblical message whatever their denominational label. "I love them, and will love them, and none shall make me do otherwise, and my house shall always be open to them all," he declared.[46] He witnessed the departure of some of his finest converts and most talented lay preachers to the Dissenters—i.e. the Congregationalists and the Baptists—without bitterness. By the end of his ministry in Haworth there were five Dissenting congregations in the locality, of which he said, "The ministers and nearly every one of the members were first awakened under my ministry."[47] In areas where there was no adequate Gospel ministry, Grimshaw encouraged the setting up of independent congregations.

A nineteenth-century drawing of Grimshaw's pulpit. Key to the eighteenth-century Evangelical Revival was preaching that centred on the great truths of the Bible.

chapter 6

Death and legacy

Grimshaw's prediction that "my stay in life will be but short" proved correct.[48] In April 1763, worn out by excessive labours, William Grimshaw succumbed to a typhus fever epidemic and died a few days later at the age of fifty-four. Speaking at his funeral service, Henry Venn called on the moors and mountains to witness "how often he was in perils by the way. …Witness, ye stormy rains and piercing colds of winter, ye fainting sultry heats of summer, how many seasons he exposed himself to your greatest inclemencies, if by any means he might save some."[49]

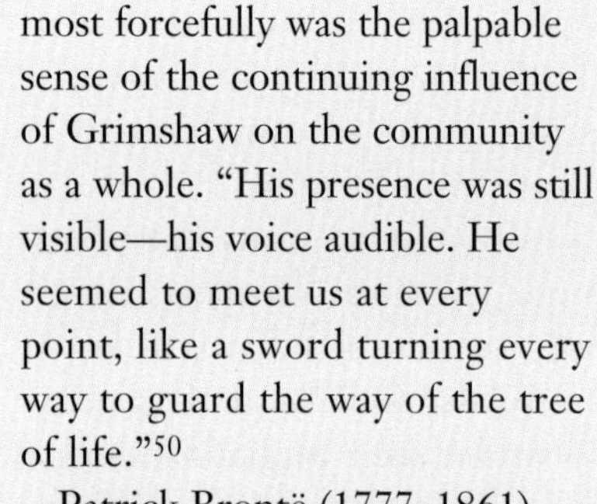

Nicknamed "the apostle of the north," the influence of Grimshaw's life and message continued long after his death in the transformed lives and habits of his parishioners. Sixty years later, in 1826, James Everett visited Haworth to collect information for a biography of Grimshaw. Some were still living who could clearly remember the colourful curate. But what struck Everett most forcefully was the palpable sense of the continuing influence of Grimshaw on the community as a whole. "His presence was still visible—his voice audible. He seemed to meet us at every point, like a sword turning every way to guard the way of the tree of life."[50]

Patrick Brontë (1777–1861), curate at the time of Everett's visit, himself espoused the same Evangelical tradition, and his daughters, yet to make Haworth famous through their literature, must have imbibed, secondhand at the very least, some of the sentiments of their father's lively predecessor. Perhaps Charlotte Brontë's famous biographer, Mrs. Gaskell, in seeking to exonerate Charlotte from the charges of vulgarity and coarseness in her novels, should have given more weight to the effect of Grimshaw's unvarnished Biblical message of sin, repentance, heaven and hell, and redemption in Christ on the Brontë sisters. "Had there been no Wesley, fire had not kindled," one writer concludes. "Had there been no Grimshaw, there would have been no fierce tale of *Wuthering Heights*."[51]

To the poet, Ted Hughes, who was brought up in neighbouring Heptonstall, Grimshaw's influence was still reverberating round his boyhood haunts in the 1930s. "To a degree," he writes, Grimshaw "changed the very landscape. His heavenly fire, straight out of Blake's *Prophetic Books*, shattered the terrain into biblical landmarks: quarries burst open like craters, and chapels—the bedrock transfigured—materialized standing in them." "Gradually it dawned on me," he concludes, "that I was living among the survivors, in the remains."[52]

(this page) The old Haworth church, exterior and interior
(opposite page) William Grimshaw

THE LIFE OF CHARLOTTE BRONTE (EDINBURGH: JOHN GRANT, 1911), FACING P.2 & FACING P.4.

appendix

William Grimshaw's letter to John Gillies

In the year 1738, our gracious Redeemer was pleased to revive his work in the West Riding, as we call it, of this county of York. Now were poor souls amongst us brought to know Jesus alone, for their wisdom, righteousness, sanctification, and redemption. The first instrument sent hither by our dear Immanuel, was one Mr. Benjamin Ingham, a clergyman, and one of the Oxford Methodists. He was born at Osset, in this Riding. The clergy at first received him into their pulpits, the churches were soon crowded, and a great stirring up of the people to seek salvation by faith alone, in the merits of a crucified Saviour, quickly appeared. But Satan, perceiving his kingdom to be in danger, began to roar, and the clergy (as I have been informed) were forbid to receive Mr. Ingham any more. Wakefield, Osset, Leeds, Halifax, and many other churches and chapels he preached in, until he was prohibited. And greatly were the people blessed. He then betook himself (as did Messrs. Wesley, Whitefield, and others at the same time) to our Saviour's manner, field preaching. As eminently did our Lord soon testify that this was his good pleasure. Multitudes assembled everywhere, and it soon appeared that conscience rather than curiosity was the main motive thereto. Man's fall and degeneracy, his redemption through Christ Jesus alone, the nature and necessity of the new birth, justification by faith only, sanctification by the indwelling Spirit of our redeemer, etc., these were (and still are) the main doctrines and subjects of all discourse. Many people not only heard, but were convinced, converted, and brought to a saving, experimental knowledge of these truths. The kingdom of God soon appeared to be a kingdom within by righteousness, and peace, and joy in the Holy Ghost....

In 1742...our dear Lord was pleased to visit my parish (Haworth). A few souls were affected under the Word, brought to see their lost estate by nature and to experience peace through faith in the blood of Jesus. My church began to be crowded, insomuch that many were obliged to stand out of doors. Here, as in other places, it was amazing to hear and see what weeping, roaring, and agonies many people were seized with at the apprehension of their sinful state and the wrath of God. After a season, I joined people (such as were truly seeking, or had found the Lord) in Society for the exercises [of praying, singing, reading, conferring together about the work of God in their souls].... These meetings here, as it is all over the kingdom, it may be your desire to understand, are held once a week, about two hours, and are called classes, consisting of about ten or twelve members each. We have much of the Lord's presence among them; and greatly, in consequence, must such meetings conduce to Christian edification. Not unto me, not unto me, but to the Lord Jesus's name solely be the praise....

What you here receive is a brief relation of the work of God in these parts of this kingdom. I suppose our brethren, particularly Mr. [John] Wesley and Mr. Whitefield, have furnished you with accounts from every other part where it hath appeared. I have only the following observations to make to you:

1. That, soon after the devil observed such crying and distress of soul and agitation of body to affect people under the Word, he also begun to seize people under the Word with strange unnatural distortions, convulsions, hideous roarings, to bring, as we plainly saw, contempt and disgrace upon the true work of God. For it is remarkable that the generality of such persons, whatsoever pretence of repentance they might then make, dwindled away to nothing.

2. That, for seven years past, the cryings and agitations in sincere penitents are in a manner ceased and are rarely seen or heard of. The Lord Jesus now carries on his work in the heart in a still serious affecting way, and I trust with as great success as ever since it began.

3. That in most places where the Gospel has been purely preached, it still flourishes, congregations increase, and doors are continually opening. Come and help us is the common cry.

4. That out of our Societies the Lord hath raised up many to preach the Gospel. None of them called thereto, but such only as are experimentally born again, and pardoned, and know the Lord Jesus Christ to be in them the hope of glory. Those speak, as our Lord says, that they do know. They speak from the heart to the heart. Their labours are wonderfully blessed. And such are God's chief instruments employed in carrying on the present wonderful work.

5. That, whereas this work took place at first mainly among the illiterate, poor, and vulgar, it, of late, has gained the credit and esteem of the more wealthy, wise, and learned sort of people. Many such, in most places, are come to experience the life, peace, and power of Christ Jesus in their souls. That so it is, is well for them indeed; but whether it presage well to the future prosperity of this work I will not say.

6. That at the first coming of the Gospel to any place, it generally happens that Satan roars, and mobs and riots are stirred up; but however violent, the Lord seldom suffers much harm to be done to his people; quietness is soon procured, and his Word takes place....

Thus you have the substance of what I can inform you of. May our very dear Saviour be with you and yours for ever. Pray for me and I'll pray for you.

W.G.

Written from Haworth, July 19, 1754. From John Gillies, *Historical Collections of Accounts of Revival* (1845 ed.; repr. Banner of Truth Trust, 1981), 506–508.

An extract from William Grimshaw's creed

I believe that Jesus is a full, as well as a free Saviour. The same yesterday, today and for ever. He alone is not only the believer's wisdom and righteousness, but his sanctification and redemption; and in Him is a fountain ever open for sin and uncleanness unto the last breath of his life. Here is my daily, necessary privilege, my relief and my comfort. …I think [that]… all that is not of faith, and consequently before faith, is sin. Nor will I allow that it is anymore by good works after grace received, than before, that a believer is saved. For however our Lord may graciously consider them at the last day, eternal life is certainly the gift of God through our Lord Jesus Christ. Christ alone has purchased for us what grace in heart and life makes us meet for. What have we to boast of? Or what have we that we have not received? Surely, by grace we are saved. When I die I shall then have my greatest grief and my greatest joy. My greatest grief that I have done so little for Jesus; and my greatest joy, that Jesus has done so much for me. My last words shall be "Here goes an unprofitable servant."[53]

Letter to William Romaine, December 8, 1762

Endnotes

[1] Ted Hughes, *Three Books: Remains of Elmet, Cave Birds, River* (London: Faber, 1993), 182. Hereafter cited as Hughes, *Three Books*.
[2] E.C. Gaskell, *The Life of Charlotte Bronte* (Edinburgh: John Grant, 1911), 18–21.
[3] James Everett, "The Curate of Haworth" (c.1825) (Manuscript in the John Rylands University Library of Manchester).
[4] For the nature of Deism, see below, p.4.
[5] *Christian Leaders of the Eighteenth Century* (Edinburgh: Banner of Truth Trust, 1978), 106–107, 146.
[6] Cited J.H. Whiteley, *Wesley's England* (London: Epworth Press, 1945), 269.
[7] Joseph Williams, Letter to Malachi Blake, March 5, 1746, cited by J.W. Laycock, *Methodist Heroes in the Great Haworth Round* (Keighley: Wadsworth & Co., 1909), 32. Hereafter cited as Laycock, *Methodist Heroes*.
[8] Cited Frank Baker, *William Grimshaw 1708–1763* (London: Epworth Press, 1963), 24. Hereafter cited as Baker, *William Grimshaw*.
[9] Benjamin Hanbury, ed., *An Enlarged Series of Extracts from the Diary, Meditations and Letters of Mr. Joseph Williams of Kidderminster* (London: C. Taylor, 1815), 225. Hereafter cited as Williams, *Diary*.
[10] John Newton, *Memoirs of the Life of Rev. William Grimshaw in Six Letters to Rev. Henry Foster* (Edinburgh: T. Hamilton, 1814), 8. Hereafter cited as Newton, *Memoirs*.
[11] Cited R. Spence Hardy, *William Grimshaw, Incumbent of Haworth* (2nd ed.; London: Mason, 1861), 20.
[12] Ibid.
[13] Everett, "The Curate of Haworth."
[14] "Experience of the Rev. Mr. Grimshaw of Haworth," *The Evangelical Magazine*, No. 2 (1794), 468–471.
[15] Williams, *Diary*, 226.
[16] Cited Henry Venn, *A Sketch of the Life and Ministry of the Late Rev. Mr. Wm. Grimshaw* (Leeds, 1763), 32. Venn preached Grimshaw's funeral sermon, at the end of which was appended this appreciative sketch of Grimshaw's life and ministry. Hereafter cited as Venn, *Sketch*.
[17] Williams, *Diary*, 226.
[18] *The Journal of the Rev. John Wesley, A.M.*, ed. Nehemiah Curnock (1909 ed.; repr. London: The Epworth Press, 1960), I, 475–476.
[19] Faith Cook, *William Grimshaw of Haworth* (Edinburgh: Banner of Truth Trust, 1997), 54–55. Hereafter cited as Cook, *Grimshaw*.
[20] J.H. Plumb, *England in the Eighteenth Century* (Harmondsworth, Middlesex: Penguin, 1950), 95.
[21] Ibid., 45.
[22] Newton, *Memoirs*, 86.
[23] Ibid., 43.
[24] "The Admonition of a Sinner" (Unpublished manuscript held in the John Rylands University Library of Manchester).
[25] Newton, *Memoirs*, 56.
[26] Cook, *Grimshaw*, 92.
[27] Ibid., 91.
[28] Ibid., 96.
[29] Ibid., 57.
[30] Ibid., 96.
[31] Ibid., 72.
[32] Williams, *Diary*, 227.
[33] Cited Cook, *Grimshaw*, 149.
[34] Ibid., 160.
[35] Ibid., 86.
[36] William Grimshaw, Letter to John Wesley, August 20, 1747 (Cook, *Grimshaw*, 300).
[37] G.R. Cragg, *Grimshaw of Haworth. A Study in Eighteenth Century Evangelicalism* (London/Edinburgh: Canterbury Press, 1947), 79.
[38] Cook, *Grimshaw*, 125.
[39] One of these communion flagons can be seen in the Brontë Museum in Haworth.
[40] *The Journal of the Rev. John Wesley, A.M.*, ed. Nehemiah Curnock (1913 ed.; repr. London: The Epworth Press, 1960), IV, 469 [entry for July 12, 1761].
[41] Cook, *Grimshaw*, 174.
[42] Letter to William Romaine, January 29, 1761 (The John Rylands University Library of Manchester).
[43] Venn, *Sketch*, 35.
[44] Letter to Mrs Gallatin, June 3, 1756 (cited Baker, *William Grimshaw*, 259).
[45] Laycock, *Methodist Heroes*, 149.
[46] Ibid., 246. See also Baker, *William Grimshaw*, 270–271.
[47] Newton, *Memoirs*, 86.
[48] Laycock, *Methodist Heroes*, 284.
[49] Venn, *Sketch*, 14.
[50] Cook, *Grimshaw*, 144.
[51] G. Elsie Harrison, *Haworth Parsonage. A Study of Wesley and the Brontës* (London: Epworth Press, 1937), 44.
[52] Hughes, *Three Books*, 182–183.
[53] The punctuation and use of capitals in the original text, cited in Cook, *Grimshaw*, 320–322, has been brought into line with early twenty-first century usage.

Heavenly Fire: William Grimshaw of Haworth

For further reading

Primary sources

John Newton, *Memoirs of the Life of Rev. William Grimshaw in Six Letters to Rev. Henry Foster* (Edinburgh: T. Hamilton, 1814).

Henry Venn, *A Sketch of the Life and Ministry of the Late Rev. Mr. Wm. Grimshaw* (Leeds, 1763), attached to his funeral sermon for Grimshaw, *Christ the Joy of the Christian's Life and Death his Gain*.

Benjamin Hanbury, ed., *An Enlarged Series of Extracts from the Diary, Meditations and Letters of Mr. Joseph Williams of Kidderminster* (London: C. Taylor, 1815).

Secondary sources

G.R. Cragg, *Grimshaw of Haworth. A Study in Eighteenth Century Evangelicalism* (London/ Edinburgh: Canterbury Press, 1947).

Faith Cook, *William Grimshaw of Haworth* (Edinburgh: Banner of Truth Trust, 1997).

Elizabeth C. Gaskell, *The Life of Charlotte Bronte* (Edinburgh: John Grant, 1911).

Ted Hughes, *Three Books: Remains of Elmet, Cave Birds, River* (London: Faber, 1993).

J.W. Laycock, *Methodist Heroes in the Great Haworth Round 1734–1784* (Keighley: Wadsworth & Co., 1909).

J.H. Plumb, *England in the Eighteenth Century* (Harmondsworth, Middlesex: Penguin Books, 1950).

J.C. Ryle, *Christian Leaders of the Eighteenth Century* (Edinburgh: Banner of Truth Trust, 1978).

A. Skevington Wood, *William Grimshaw of Haworth* (London: The Evangelical Library, 1963).

Acknowledgements

The publishers wish to thank Faith Cook, Penny Dickson and Steven Wood for their assistance in the production of this book.

About the author

Esther Bennett has a degree in history from Cambridge University where she received a prize for her work on eighteenth-century church history. She is married and has three daughters.